Same-Sex Marriage

Obergefell v. Hodges

GERRY BOEHME

Cavendish
Square

New York

30910 3115
C

Published in 2019 by Cavendish Square Publishing, LLC
243 5th Avenue, Suite 136, New York, NY 10016

Copyright © 2019 by Cavendish Square Publishing, LLC

First Edition

No part of this publication may be reproduced, stored in a retrieval system, or transmitted in any form or by any means—electronic, mechanical, photocopying, recording, or otherwise—without the prior permission of the copyright owner. Request for permission should be addressed to Permissions, Cavendish Square Publishing, 243 5th Avenue, Suite 136, New York, NY 10016. Tel (877) 980-4450; fax (877) 980-4454.

Website: cavendishsq.com

This publication represents the opinions and views of the author based on his or her personal experience, knowledge, and research. The information in this book serves as a general guide only. The author and publisher have used their best efforts in preparing this book and disclaim liability rising directly or indirectly from the use and application of this book.

All websites were available and accurate when this book was sent to press.

Library of Congress Cataloging-in-Publication Data

Names: Boehme, Gerry, author.
Title: Same-sex marriage : Obergefell v. Hodges / Gerry Boehme.
Description: New York : Cavendish Square, 2018. | Series: Courting
history | Includes bibliographical references and index.
Identifiers: LCCN 2018002363 (print) | LCCN 2018002932
(ebook) | ISBN 9781502635938 (ebook) | ISBN 9781502635921
(library bound) | ISBN 9781502635945 (pbk.)
Subjects: LCSH: Obergefell, James--Trials, litigation, etc.--Juvenile literature. |
Same-sex marriage--Law and legislation--United States--Juvenile literature. |
Gay couples--Legal status, laws, etc.--United States--Juvenile literature.
Classification: LCC KF229.O24 (ebook) | LCC KF229.
O24 B64 2018 (print) | DDC 346.7301/68--dc23
LC record available at https://lccn.loc.gov/2018002363

Editorial Director: David McNamara
Editor: Chet'la Sebree
Copy Editor: Nathan Heidelberger
Associate Art Director: Amy Greenan
Designer: Joseph Parenteau
Production Coordinator: Karol Szymczuk
Photo Research: J8 Media

Printed in the United States of America

Contents

ONE
First Steps to Equality

In 1992, two men, Jim Obergefell and John Arthur, fell in love.

Jim Obergefell was from Sandusky, Ohio. John Arthur hailed from Chicago, Illinois. Both men attended college at the University of Cincinnati in Ohio. They did not meet until they were introduced by friends in 1992. Later that year, Jim and John decided that they wanted to spend their lives together.

In 1993, Jim Obergefell moved to Cincinnati, where Arthur lived. They soon bought a home. For the next twenty years, Obergefell and Arthur built a happy life. Both men had good careers, and they enjoyed traveling all over the world. Like other couples in love, Jim Obergefell and John Arthur also wanted to get married.

Unlike opposite-sex couples, however, Jim and John could not legally marry. Like many other states at that time, Ohio had passed laws forbidding marriage between people of the same sex.

Unequal Treatment

Throughout history, there have been times when people tried to limit the freedoms of others who were different. The United States Declaration of Independence includes

Jim Obergefell (*left*) and John Arthur (*right*) went to court to change Ohio's law against same-sex marriage.

the phrase "We hold these truths to be self-evident, that all men are created equal." In other words, the writers of the Declaration of Independence thought it was obvious that all people are equals. However, even back then people disagreed about what the term "all men" really meant.

When America was founded, only wealthy men could vote, and slavery was legal. As the country followed a long and sometimes painful path toward equality for all its citizens, many of these past injustices were eventually swept away. The Emancipation Proclamation officially ended slavery in the United States in 1863. In 1920, the Nineteenth Amendment to the US Constitution granted American women the right to vote.

5

Since then, other groups of Americans have continued their own struggles for equal rights. Although slavery ended in the 1800s, racial discrimination, or the unfair treatment of someone based on their race, continued into the twentieth century. During the 1950s and 1960s, African American leaders like Martin Luther King Jr. and John Lewis organized protests against racial discrimination. These protests helped pass the Civil Rights Act of 1964. Even after the act was passed, however, some areas of the country still discriminated against African Americans. For instance, African Americans were not allowed to marry someone who was white. Over time, many of these practices were also struck down by the government or by US courts.

Marriage Between Races

In 1958, two people in Virginia, Mildred Jeter and Richard Loving, wanted to get married. Mildred was African American. Richard was white. At that time, it was against the law for a man and a woman of two different races to get married in Virginia. Since this was the law, Jeter and Loving legally married in the District of Columbia. When they returned to Virginia, however, they were arrested and later found guilty.

Jeter and Loving avoided jail by moving to Washington, DC. However, they filed a lawsuit against the state of Virginia in 1963. The case eventually reached the US Supreme Court. In its unanimous 1967 decision *Loving v. Virginia*, the Supreme Court struck down Virginia's law against interracial marriage, along with all similar laws in other states. Chief Justice Earl Warren wrote that "under our Constitution, the freedom to marry, or not marry, a person

6

Mildred Jeter and Richard Loving won the Supreme Court case that overturned Virginia's law against interracial marriage.

of another race resides with the individual, and cannot be infringed by the State." In other words, Justice Warren believed it was an individual's right to make a decision about whom he or she wanted to marry.

While *Loving v. Virginia* legalized interracial marriage, it would take almost another half century before same-sex couples could claim the same victory.

Same-Sex Couples

An opposite-sex, or heterosexual, couple is made up of a woman and a man. A homosexual, or same-sex, couple is either made up of two women or two men. People in same-sex relationships, also known as homosexuals, have faced discrimination in society. At times in the United States, they could not be teachers, join the army, or be lawyers or doctors.

7

They also could not marry someone they loved if they were the same sex.

Some people feel morally opposed to homosexuality, and others consider it to be a disease. In 1974, the American Psychiatric Association debunked the belief that homosexuality was a disease. Since then, many states have passed laws to protect the rights of people who love others of the same sex. Some organizations and religions allow same-sex couples to wed. However, no US state permitted two people of the same sex to legally marry until Massachusetts changed its laws in 2004.

The Beginning of Change

Same-sex couples began to take steps to have society accept their relationships like those between men and women. In many ways, these same-sex couples followed the earlier paths of women and African Americans who had won their own rights to equal treatment. Some same-sex couples organized public protests and election campaigns. Others turned to the legal system. They hired attorneys and asked the courts to change policies that prevented same-sex couples from receiving equal treatment under the law.

Over the years, both sides experienced their share of victories and defeats. In 1972, the Minnesota Supreme Court ruled that marriage should remain "a union of man and woman" (*Baker v. Nelson*). In 1993, however, the Supreme Court of Hawaii ruled that the state had to present strong evidence to support its law against same-sex marriage (*Baehr v. Lewin*). That decision and others made people question whether states could ban same-sex marriages. These questions led the US Congress to pass the Defense of Marriage Act

(DOMA) in 1996. The act defined marriage as being between a man and a woman.

When DOMA passed, many states felt more confident to pass their own laws against same-sex marriage and against recognizing those performed in other states. By 2001, forty-one states had passed these kinds of laws or amendments. In November 2008, California voters approved Proposition 8. This law banned same-sex marriage in that state.

Illness Leads to Action

Even though Obergefell and Arthur could not get married, they lived together happily for many years. However, in 2011, Arthur began to have trouble walking and performing other normal physical acts. After medical tests, the couple learned that Arthur had amyotrophic lateral sclerosis (ALS). ALS is a deadly disease that eventually robs a person of the ability to walk and even to breathe. ALS is always fatal, and there is no known cure.

Arthur's illness made the couple want to get married even more than before. They both knew that Arthur would soon pass away. They wanted his death certificate to list him as married, with Obergefell as his legal spouse. They also wanted Obergefell to receive the same rights that other surviving spouses in Ohio receive.

Time to Get Married

On June 26, 2013, the US Supreme Court decided two cases that forever changed the way that Americans viewed same-sex couples. In *United States v. Windsor*, the Supreme Court ruled that part of DOMA was unconstitutional. This decision meant that the federal government had to recognize same-sex

The Defeat of DOMA

In 1996, Bob Barr, a Republican congressman from Georgia, introduced a law. That law became known as the Defense of Marriage Act (DOMA). DOMA defined marriage as "only a legal union between one man and one woman as husband and wife." The act allowed states to refuse to recognize same-sex marriages from other states. It also denied same-sex spouses benefits that the federal government gave to married couples.

At that time, it was up to each state to pass laws about marriage. They could decide who could wed and how the ceremony could be conducted. After DOMA was signed into law on September 21, 1996, many states across the country decided to limit or ban same-sex marriage.

Bob Barr fought against same-sex marriage but later changed his mind.

Bob Barr eventually regretted sponsoring DOMA. "I apologize for that," he said in 2008. "[The] Defense of Marriage Act ... provided the federal government a club to club down the rights of law-abiding American citizens ... and should be repealed." In other words, he realized that DOMA gave the government the power to take away people's rights. Barr thought this was wrong.

When the US Supreme Court struck down sections of DOMA in 2013, it removed the federal government's power to make decisions about the legality of a marriage. The court maintained that the power to define marriage belonged to individual states.

marriages. On the same day, the court overturned California's Proposition 8 that had banned same-sex marriages in that state (*Hollingsworth v. Perry*).

After the Supreme Court decisions, Jim Obergefell and John Arthur decided it was time to challenge Ohio's policy on same-sex marriage. Ohio banned same-sex marriages and refused to recognize those that were performed in other states. Obergefell and Arthur realized it might take too long to change the ban on same-sex marriage. However, they thought they might be able to get Ohio to recognize marriages performed in other states.

Edith Windsor's victory in *United States v. Windsor* granted same-sex married couples federal recognition.

Obergefell sent an email to Arthur's aunt Paulette Roberts. Obergefell told Roberts that he had asked Arthur to marry him "as soon as the Supreme Court ruled DOMA unconstitutional." He wanted Roberts to officiate their ceremony. She had already become a minister in hopes of doing just that.

One short plane ride later, Obergefell and Arthur took their first steps toward changing policies and attitudes about same-sex marriage across the entire country.

TWO
The Road to the Supreme Court

Obergefell and Arthur decided to get married in Maryland. At the time, it was one of thirteen states that permitted same-sex marriages. Once they were married, Obergefell and Arthur returned home to Cincinnati. They planned to ask Ohio to accept their Maryland marriage license.

Why did Obergefell and Arthur feel so strongly about Ohio recognizing their marriage? The couple felt that their loving relationship should receive the same public acceptance as marriages between men and women. However, they also had other important reasons for trying to change Ohio's policy.

Marriage Benefits

While many marriages include a religious ceremony, all marriages also involve a legal contract. These contracts provide married couples with important federal and state benefits. Married couples have equal rights as parents and can adopt children more easily. They can own property together and share government benefits. They also save money on insurance and pay lower taxes. A married person can also make important decisions for his or her spouse such as arranging for hospital care and making funeral arrangements.

12

After John Arthur died, Jim Obergefell combined their wedding rings to show they would always be together.

Arthur knew that he would soon pass away. He wanted his death certificate to clearly state that he was married to Obergefell. Additionally, Arthur wanted to be buried in his family's cemetery plot, which included spouses. Obergefell could not be buried with Arthur when he died if they were not legally married.

Suing for Recognition

One week after their Maryland marriage, on July 19, 2013, Obergefell and Arthur filed a federal lawsuit in the United States District Court for the Southern District of Ohio. Their lawsuit challenged Ohio's ban on same-sex marriages.

District courts are the first of three levels within the federal court system. District courts handle criminal cases. Criminal cases are ones in which the government accuses someone of breaking the law. The district courts also handle civil cases. Those are cases where one person sues another due to a personal dispute. At least one district court exists in each state.

The losing side in a district court case can appeal to a higher court called a court of appeals. Filing an appeal means the losing side asks a higher court to change a lower court's ruling. There are thirteen courts of appeals in the country. Each one covers a particular region, called a circuit. Ohio is covered by the US Court of Appeals for the Sixth Circuit, which also handles Kentucky, Michigan, and Tennessee. A court of appeals can uphold, or agree with, a district court ruling, or it can strike the ruling down.

The losing side in a court of appeals decision can appeal to the US Supreme Court, the highest court in the country.

Obergefell and Arthur hired Al Gerhardstein to handle their case. Gerhardstein was a Cincinnati civil rights lawyer who supported same-sex marriage. Obergefell, Arthur, and Gerhardstein felt that their best chance at winning the lawsuit would be to focus only on making Ohio recognize the Maryland marriage license. The state already recognized some marriages performed elsewhere that were forbidden under Ohio law. For instance, Ohio recognized marriages between first cousins or minors performed in other states. Therefore, Gerhardstein argued, Ohio's refusal to accept out-of-state same-sex marriages treated same-sex couples differently than other couples. This difference in treatment violated the equal protection clause of the US Constitution. The equal protection clause guarantees that all US citizens are treated the same way under the law.

Gerhardstein also used the *Windsor* decision in his argument. The Supreme Court had declared that part of the

Civil rights lawyer Al Gerhardstein argued that Ohio should accept same-sex marriages performed in other states.

Defense of Marriage Act was unconstitutional. Gerhardstein argued that the *Windsor* verdict meant that legal marriages from one state should be "portable," or carried over, to other states. In addition, Gerhardstein told the court that the couple would face "irreparable harm" if Ohio refused to list Arthur as married on his death certificate. In other words, the damage could not be undone.

On July 22, 2013, Judge Timothy Black granted a restraining order that prevented Ohio from issuing a death certificate that listed Arthur as unmarried.

Others Join

On September 26, two more plaintiffs, or people who bring a case against other people, joined the lawsuit. These two people were David Michener and Robert Grunn. Michener also lived in Cincinnati. Earlier in 2013, he had married another man, William Ives, in Delaware. Ives had recently died. Like Obergefell, Michener wanted to be legally recognized as Ives's surviving spouse. Robert Grunn owned a Cincinnati funeral home. He planned to list same-sex spouses when he filled out death certificates. However, Grunn feared he would be arrested unless Ohio's law changed.

Arthur Dies

John Arthur passed away on October 22, 2013. Obergefell decided to continue the lawsuit. It had now been amended, or changed, to include Obergefell, Michener, and Grunn as co-plaintiffs. In lawsuits of this type, the plaintiffs usually name as defendants the people in charge of the government departments that enforce the law they want to change. Defendants are the people who are being sued or accused of a crime. The amended case named Dr. Theodore Wymyslo as a defendant: *Obergefell v. Wymyslo.* At the time, he was the director of the Ohio Department of Health.

Victories and Appeals

On December 23, 2013, Judge Timothy Black ruled in favor of the plaintiffs. He decided that Ohio had to recognize out-of-state same-sex marriages on death certificates. To explain his decision, Black wrote that "the right to remain married is recognized as a fundamental liberty interest protected by the Due Process Clause of the United States Constitution." The due process clause prohibits states from taking away individuals' rights without a fair trial. Black also said that Ohio "treating lawful same-sex marriages differently than it treats lawful opposite sex marriages … violates the United States Constitution's guarantee of equal protection." In other words,

Judge Timothy Black ruled in favor of Obergefell and other plaintiffs at the Potter Stewart Courthouse in Cincinnati, Ohio.

Black believed that Ohio was violating people's constitutional rights by not recognizing their marriage licenses.

However, Judge Black's decision only applied to death certificates. Despite that fact, other couples soon tried to use his district court ruling as a precedent to expand state policies. A precedent is when a decision in an earlier legal case is used as an example or guide to make a decision in a similar case in the future. Shortly after Black's decision, four same-sex couples joined together to file a different lawsuit. They sued against Ohio's law that prevented them from listing both of their names as parents on a child's birth certificate. Their case was called *Henry v. Wymyslo*.

On April 14, 2014, Judge Black ruled in favor of those couples. Black also declared that Ohio's policy of not recognizing out-of-state same-sex marriages was unconstitutional. However, he decided not to require Ohio

A Change of Heart

Democrats and Republicans often disagree on many social issues, including same-sex marriage. During Obergefell's case, Democratic leaders like Senator Harry Reid and Congresswoman Nancy Pelosi supported marriage for same-sex couples. Meanwhile, top Republicans like Senator Mitch McConnell and Congressman John Boehner opposed it.

President Obama expressed his support of same-sex marriage during a 2012 interview with Robin Roberts of ABC's *Good Morning America*.

However, politicians' feelings about same-sex marriage did not just follow political party lines. For instance, Democrat Barack Obama did not support same-sex marriage initially. Just before he was elected president in November 2008, Obama told an MTV audience "I believe marriage is between a man and a woman."

In May 2012, however, President Obama switched positions. He credited his two daughters for helping change his mind. In an interview, he talked about how his daughters had friends whose parents were same-sex couples. He said he did not know how he would explain to his daughters that their friends' parents would be treated differently in the eyes of the law. For that reason, he changed his position about same-sex marriage.

to immediately change its policies. He gave the state time to appeal to a higher court.

In January 2014, Ohio had filed its appeal of *Obergefell* with the Court of Appeals for the Sixth Circuit. In May, the state appealed Judge Black's decision in the *Henry* case as well, and the two cases were combined. Later that year, Richard Hodges took over as the new director of the Ohio Department of Health. The case was again amended and renamed *Obergefell v. Hodges*.

Ohio was not the only state facing lawsuits over same-sex marriage. In 2014, same-sex couples in Michigan and Tennessee sued those states to allow them to jointly adopt children. That same year, four same-sex couples challenged Kentucky's law against recognizing out-of-state marriages. They argued that the law prevented them from receiving marriage benefits. In all these cases, judges used Judge Black's decision as a precedent to declare laws in those states unconstitutional.

Similar to Black, judges in these other cases often issued stays, or short delays, to give the defendant time before obeying the court's decision. These stays allowed the states to delay changing their policies while they appealed to a higher court.

Reversal

Ohio, Tennessee, Kentucky and Michigan all fell under the jurisdiction of the Court of Appeals for the Sixth Circuit. All of these states filed appeals of the district court decisions. On August 6, 2014, the court heard arguments for all the cases: *Obergefell v. Hodges* (from Ohio, combined with the *Henry* case), *Bourke v. Beshear* (Kentucky, combined with another case, *Love v. Beshear*), *Tanco v. Haslam* (Tennessee) and *DeBoer v. Snyder* (Michigan).

On November 6, 2014, three appeals court judges reversed the lower courts' rulings. They voted 2–1 in favor of the states. In other words, they upheld the positions the states took on same-sex marriage. In their ruling, the judges said that state laws against same-sex marriage did not violate the US Constitution. They believed that it should be up to state voters and lawmakers to decide the legality of same-sex marriage.

The Next Fight

Obergefell and the other same-sex couples may have lost this latest battle, but the fight was not over. Their next move would forever change the laws surrounding same-sex marriage in the United States.

THREE

Making the Case

When the Court of Appeals for the Sixth Circuit reversed the lower court rulings, Obergefell and his legal team had to make a choice. They could ask for another hearing at the court of appeals in front of all sixteen judges. Alternatively, they could appeal directly to the US Supreme Court.

Obergefell and the other plaintiffs decided not to wait. On November 14, 2014, they filed a petition for writ of certiorari with the US Supreme Court. A petition for a writ of certiorari means that a losing side in a case asks the highest court in the country to review it. The writ of certiorari is a document from the Supreme Court stating that it will hear the case.

Against the Odds

It's not easy to get the Supreme Court to accept a case. At least four out of the nine Supreme Court justices have to recommend that the case be reviewed. The cases they choose usually deal with important issues about the US Constitution or federal law. Each year, the US Supreme Court receives more than 7,000 requests to review cases. It usually accepts fewer than 150. It only grants full hearings to about 80.

Obergefell and the other plaintiffs felt that they had many good reasons for the Supreme Court to accept their case.

Same-Sex Marriage:
Obergefell v. Hodges

Federal judge Deborah Cook of the Court of Appeals for the Sixth Circuit voted to overturn Judge Black's decision in *Obergefell.*

They had won decisions in four different states before the court of appeals overturned those rulings. The appeals court's reversal also went against decisions made by four other courts of appeals in the country. These other courts ruled that state bans on same-sex marriages were unconstitutional. Also, the Court of Appeals for the Sixth Circuit voted 2–1. This close vote was another reason the Supreme Court might review the case.

The plaintiffs also knew that people's attitudes about same-sex marriage were changing. The Supreme Court had recently supported several lower court decisions that overturned state laws against same-sex marriage. Additionally, thirty-six states at the time granted marriage licenses to same-sex couples.

However, fourteen states still refused. The subject continued to divide Americans across the country. Many people wanted the Supreme Court to decide the issue once and for all. They wanted the court to establish a policy for the entire nation.

On January 16, 2015, the Supreme Court announced that it would hear *Obergefell v. Hodges.* The review would combine the cases from all four states: Ohio, Kentucky, Tennessee, and Michigan. It would include forty-two individual plaintiffs.

The justices who decided *Obergefell*: (*clockwise from top left*) Sotomayor, Breyer, Alito, Kagan, Ginsburg, Kennedy, Roberts, Scalia, and Thomas

Different Philosophies

Supreme Court justices are supposed to be impartial, or neutral. They are supposed to make all of their decisions according to the law. However, the justices can be influenced by their beliefs and backgrounds just like other people.

The nine Supreme Court justices that would hear the *Obergefell* case came from different backgrounds. Chief Justice John Roberts and Justices Samuel Alito, Antonin Scalia, and Clarence Thomas had all been appointed by Republican presidents. These justices were considered to be more conservative and traditional in nature. Justices Ruth Bader Ginsburg, Sonia Sotomayor, Elena Kagan, and Stephen Breyer had all been appointed by Democrats. They were thought to be more liberal and accepting of change.

The ninth justice was Anthony Kennedy. He had been selected by a Republican president like the more conservative justices. However, he had voted to expand same-sex rights in

several Supreme Court decisions. When the court decided
to hear *Obergefell*, many legal experts predicted that the four
liberal justices would probably support the plaintiffs. They
also believed that the four conservative justices would favor
the states. That would leave Justice Kennedy to provide the
swing vote, or the vote that decides a close case that could
"swing" one way or the other.

Written and Oral Arguments

When the Supreme Court considers a case, the first step is
for each side to submit a short, written summary, called a
legal brief. The brief talks about the issues of the case and
how they relate to the current laws. The justices read the
briefs to become familiar with the case's arguments.

After the briefs are submitted and reviewed, attorneys
from each side get the opportunity to speak before the court.
These oral arguments give the justices and the public a

People from both sides demonstrated in front of the Supreme Court during
the *Obergefell v. Hodges* case.

chance to hear the lawyers from each side support their case. During oral arguments, the justices can also ask the attorneys questions about what they said and what they have written in their briefs.

The briefs in *Obergefell* were focused on two questions. The first question was whether or not a state was required by the Fourteenth Amendment to issue a marriage license to two people of the same sex. The second question was whether or not a state was required by the Fourteenth Amendment to recognize marriage licenses issued by different states to two people of the same sex.

Outside Interests

On February 27, 2015, the lawyers supporting same-sex marriage submitted their written briefs. Lawyers for the states submitted theirs on March 27. The petitioners, or plaintiffs in this case, then submitted responses to the state briefs on April 17.

Many other people and organizations also felt strongly about the case. They filed amicus curiae, or "friend-of-the-court," briefs. These people included law professors, members of Congress, representatives from other states, and political and religious organizations. The US government submitted its own brief supporting the petitioners on March 6.

The Plaintiffs' Attorneys and Their Case

The Supreme Court scheduled oral arguments to take place on April 28, 2015. The plaintiffs chose civil rights attorney Mary Bonauto to represent them. Bonauto had represented April DeBoer, one of the plaintiffs, in the adoption case from Michigan. Bonauto was responsible for arguing whether or

A Long-Time Advocate

Attorney Mary Bonauto worked for many years to support same-sex marriage before she addressed the Supreme Court in *Obergefell v. Hodges*.

Beginning in 1990, Bonauto worked on civil rights issues for GLAD (GLBTQ Legal Advocates and Defenders). This organization defends GLBTQ, or LGBTQ, rights. LGBTQ stands for "lesbian, gay, bisexual, transgender, and queer." Through GLAD, Bonauto represented same-sex couples in many important cases, including *Goodridge v. Department of Public Health* in 2003. That case led directly to Massachusetts becoming the first state to legalize same-sex marriage in 2004. Bonauto also helped GLAD challenge DOMA. Many people credit Bonauto with helping develop a long-term strategy for legalizing same-sex marriage.

Mary Bonauto convinced the justices to rule in favor of same-sex marriage.

Bonauto continued to fight for equality after the *Obergefell v. Hodges* case. In June 2016, she told the *Boston Globe* that she is working toward a "world in which there are no impediments to people's opportunities and freedoms because of who they are or who they love."

not states should license same-sex marriages. The plaintiffs also selected Douglas Hallward-Driemeier as an attorney. He had argued on behalf of one of the Tennessee plaintiffs. He was responsible for arguing that states should recognize same-sex marriages legally performed in other states. The petitioners also asked the court to allow the solicitor general, or the attorney responsible for arguing cases to the Supreme Court on behalf of the federal government, to speak. At the time, the US solicitor general was Donald B. Verrilli.

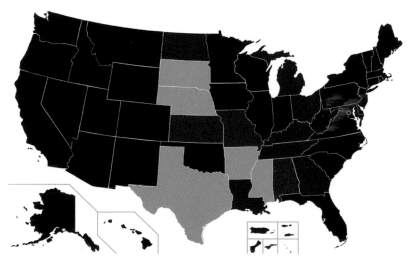

While many states allowed same-sex marriages (blue) before *Obergefell*, other states banned (red) or disputed the legality (purple and yellow) of same-sex marriages until the Supreme Court ruling.

The petitioners argued that same-sex couples were simply seeking equal treatment for an existing, "fundamental" right. They just wanted to be married like other couples. They said this right was covered by the Fourteenth Amendment's equal protection and due process clauses. The equal protection clause guarantees that all laws and rights are applied to US citizens equally. The due process clause says that a state cannot take away a US citizen's rights without fair treatment in the court system. The plaintiffs were arguing that same-sex couples were not given the fundamental right to marry. They also were not treated equally by the courts.

During her oral presentation, Mary Bonauto argued that the US Constitution guaranteed same-sex couples the "legal commitment, responsibility, and protection that is marriage." It was a fundamental right of all US citizens. She argued that state laws had to respect people's rights under the Constitution. Chief Justice Roberts claimed that same-sex couples were not "seeking to join the institution [of marriage]." He thought they were "seeking to change what the institution is." To Roberts, marriage was a union between a man and a woman. Bonauto answered that the Fourteenth Amendment provided "enduring guarantees" of equality, even if some states viewed marriage differently.

Justice Kennedy asked whether the movement for same-sex marriage should slow down. He thought it may take more time for people to change their ideas about marriage. "The definition [of marriage] has been with us for millennia," Kennedy said. He thought it was "very difficult for the court to say oh, well, … we know better." Justice Breyer echoed Kennedy's concerns. He said that the idea of marriage between a man and a woman "has been the law everywhere for thousands of years." He thought it would be hard for "nine people outside the ballot box to require states that don't want to do it to change [that]." In other words, he thought that this decision should be left up to the states as opposed to the nine Supreme Court justices.

The court asked Bonauto if states' voters should make decisions about same-sex marriage. Bonauto answered that

that slow pace of change would be harmful to couples and children who would have to wait even longer to be accepted. "Waiting is not neutral," she said. She meant that waiting had a real effect on certain people's lives. She also argued that it should be up to "the individual to decide who to marry." Solicitor General Verrilli echoed that point when he presented his oral argument.

Jayne Rowse (*second from left*) and April DeBoer (*right*) went to court in Michigan so they could jointly adopt each other's children.

Bonauto argued that ideas about marriage had already changed over time. Women had won equal status in marriage. Laws against interracial marriage had been struck down. After those laws changed, people realized that it should have been done sooner.

When it was Hallward-Driemeier's turn to speak, he brought up the way that states recognized out-of-state marriages of heterosexual couples. He argued that the states' refusal to recognize out-of-state same-sex marriages was "a

stark departure." Justice Roberts challenged this. He asked
if one state performed a marriage that had to be accepted in
every other state, wouldn't that mean that one state could set
policy for the entire country? Hallward-Driemeier answered
that if one state allows same-sex couples to establish
relationships and families under the protection of the law,
then other states should not be allowed to destroy those
marriages with their own local laws.

The Defendants' Attorneys and Their Case

The defendants chose John J. Bursch as their attorney. Bursh
was the Special Assistant Attorney General for the state of
Michigan. He defended states' rights to decide whether or
not to recognize same-sex marriage licenses from other states.
He also defended states' rights to ban same-sex marriages.

Bursch also discussed his understanding of marriage
and family. He believed married couples were supposed to
procreate, or physically have children. Heterosexual couples
could do this, while same-sex couples could not. He also
believed that parents of opposite sexes complemented each
other and contributed different qualities to a family with
children. In other words, he thought children benefited from
being raised by one man and one woman. He used these
arguments as part of his defense.

Bursch supported his argument by stating that the
Fourteenth Amendment did not define what marriage was.
According to Bursch, anything not specifically outlined in
the Fourteenth Amendment should be left to the states to
decide. This stance was similar to the position that attorneys
had taken decades earlier when defending interracial
marriage bans.

Even though Bursch explained his feelings about marriage, he did not believe the case should be "about how to define marriage." He thought the case should be about "who gets to decide that question." He did not believe the federal courts should make that decision. He thought individual people with voting rights in each state should make the decision. Bursch thought that was more democratic.

Justice Breyer compared Bursch's stance to the stance states had taken in the fight against racial discrimination. If the Supreme Court used Bursch's stance, then it would have never found interracial marriage bans or racial segregation unconstitutional.

Associate Solicitor General Joseph Whalen of Tennessee was also an attorney for the defense. He argued the second question about whether or not states should be required to recognize same-sex marriages performed in other states. He argued that it was important for a state to maintain a "cohesive and coherent ... policy with regard to marriage." In other words, it would make sense for a state that bans same-sex marriages to also not recognize same-sex marriages performed in other states. Like Bursch, he also talked about states' rights. He believed that the court should accept that states have different points of view based on their residents' feelings.

The Wait Begins

After the oral presentations ended, the nine Supreme Court justices left the public eye to consider the arguments. It would take nearly two months before they would announce their landmark decision.

FOUR

Recognition

After the arguments ended on April 28, people began to review the written briefs, the oral presentations, and the justices' questions and comments. They were trying to get a feel for how the justices might rule in *Obergefell v. Hodges*.

The stakes were high. The justices could decide that state laws against same-sex marriage violated the US Constitution. If that happened, every state would have to treat same-sex couples the same as opposite-sex couples. On the other hand, the court could uphold the bans. If that happened, other states that already approved same-sex

Jim Obergefell finally claimed victory after the US Supreme Court legalized same-sex marriage.

marriage might change their minds. The progress that same-sex couples had struggled for could be reversed.

After the hearing closed, most observers still believed that the four conservative judges (Roberts, Scalia, Thomas, and Alito) seemed to favor the states. They also believed the four liberal justices (Breyer, Kagan, Sotomayor, and Ginsburg) supported the petitioners. As many had predicted before the case began, the judgment for or against same-sex marriage would probably hinge on Justice Anthony Kennedy's swing vote.

No Set Pattern

Anthony Kennedy had been appointed to the Supreme Court by President Ronald Reagan in 1987. Although he had been appointed by a Republican president, Kennedy did not make court decisions based on his religious or political beliefs. He made his decisions based on the merits of each individual

Jim Obergefell held a photo of his late husband, John Arthur, when he spoke to the media after winning *Obergefell v. Hodges.*

case. During his more than twenty-five years on the Supreme Court, Kennedy sided with both his more liberal and his more conservative colleagues.

One thing that Kennedy seemed to consistently support was equal rights for all people. He had already written important opinions supporting LGBTQ rights in 1996, 2003, and 2013. Kennedy also frequently used the term "dignity" when referring to marriage. He thought same-sex marriages deserved the states' respect. Attorneys representing both sides in *Obergefell v. Hodges* knew how much Kennedy valued the idea of dignity. They all made sure to include that word in their written briefs and oral arguments.

Obergefell Wins

On June 26, 2015, the US Supreme Court announced its decision. In a 5–4 vote, the court overturned the appeals court's ruling. The Supreme Court ruled in favor of Jim Obergefell and the other plaintiffs. The close decision reflected the divisions among the states and the American population.

In its decision, the court ruled that the Fourteenth Amendment did indeed guarantee marriage equality. The decision meant that all states had to allow same-sex couples to marry. It also meant that all states had to recognize same-sex marriages that took place in other states. The ruling also protected same-sex couples who had already been married, since some states had put legal acceptance on hold until the Supreme Court ruled on the case.

Justice Anthony Kennedy had indeed provided the swing vote that broke a tie between the conservative and liberal justices. In fact, Justice Kennedy wrote the majority opinion, or written explanation for a decision that more than half of the judges of a court have agreed on. Kennedy's opinion explained why the court voted to support the right of same-sex couples to marry. As many expected, Justice Kennedy referred to personal dignity in his opinion. In fact, he used the word "dignity" nine times.

An Existing Right

Kennedy wrote that preventing same-sex couples from marrying denied them the equal protection that is guaranteed in the Fourteenth Amendment. He explained that the Supreme Court was not granting same-sex couples a "new

How the Supreme Court Justices Voted in *Obergefell v. Hodges*

Question 1: Does the Fourteenth Amendment require a state to license a marriage between two people of the same sex?
Yes: Kennedy, Ginsburg, Breyer, Kagan, Sotomayor
No: Roberts, Alito, Scalia, Thomas

Question 2: Does the Fourteenth Amendment require a state to recognize a marriage between two people of the same sex that was legally licensed and performed in another state?
Yes: Kennedy, Ginsburg, Breyer, Kagan, Sotomayor
No: Roberts, Alito, Scalia, Thomas

right" to marry. The court
decision simply extended an
existing right to same-sex
couples who had been unfairly
prevented from being married.

Justice Kennedy's opinion
emphasized the importance
of marriage. He wrote that
marriage "allows two people
to find a life that could not
be found alone." He went
on to write that "marriage is
essential to our most profound

Kennedy provided the swing vote
and wrote the majority opinion.

hopes and aspirations." In other words, he thought marriage
was not just a right but a need of most people. He thought it
wrong and illegal to deprive anyone of that.

He also went on to talk about how same-sex couples did
not want to insult the institution of marriage. In his opinion,
he wrote:

> It would misunderstand these men and women to say
> they disrespect the idea of marriage. Their plea is that
> they do respect it, respect it so deeply that they seek to
> find its fulfillment for themselves. Their hope is not to
> be condemned to live in loneliness, excluded from one
> of civilization's oldest institutions. They ask for equal
> dignity in the eyes of the law.

In other words, Kennedy saw marriage as the joining of
love. He understood that same-sex couples were hoping to
legally participate in one of the oldest ways we recognize love.

Kennedy also mentioned the due process clause of the
Fourteenth Amendment in the majority opinion. The clause

says no state shall "deprive any person of life, liberty, or property, without due process of law." Kennedy wrote that "the fundamental liberties protected by this Clause include ... certain personal choices central to individual dignity and autonomy." In other words, he thought someone's decision about whom to marry was a right protected by the due process clause. He did not believe states could take away that right.

The court made it clear that it should not be left to the voters in each state to decide the legality of same-sex marriage. Kennedy and the justices in the majority believed "fundamental rights may not be submitted to a vote." In other words, people in individual states should not be allowed to decide if citizens are entitled to federally protected rights.

Although Kennedy wrote a strong opinion, he acknowledged people who did not support his position. Kennedy realized that some people wanted same-sex marriage efforts to slow down until opponents were more comfortable with the idea. In response, Kennedy brought up same-sex couples who wanted to raise their children together. He believed that if they were forced to wait, "the childhood years will pass all too soon." Like Bonauto in her oral argument, Kennedy acknowledged that waiting had real consequences for real people.

Justice Kennedy still tried to be sensitive to the opposition. He knew people who believed that marriage should be only between a man and a woman might still oppose same-sex marriage. He believed that the debate should continue. He thought those with religious views on the subject should be protected by the First Amendment. That amendment "ensures that religious organizations and persons are given proper protection as they seek to teach the

Supporters of same-sex marriage celebrated their victory in front of the Supreme Court.

principles that are so fulfilling and so central to their lives and faiths." However, in the meantime, he believed same-sex marriages must be allowed.

No Rule Book

According to some people, since the US Constitution did not specifically define marriage, the states were within their rights to define it. Justice Kennedy did not agree. He argued that America's founders could not anticipate every issue that would occur in the future. He believed the founders intended for the laws and their interpretations to evolve over time.

As an example, Kennedy pointed to the 1967 Supreme Court decision in *Loving v. Virginia*. Interracial couples were granted the constitutional right to marry, although some people believed they shouldn't. Kennedy also cited several other important Supreme Court decisions that showed how society had changed its views on love and marriage.

Courts Should Not Make Laws

Chief Justice Roberts wrote the dissenting opinion for the four justices who voted against the plaintiffs. A dissenting opinion is a written statement for the justices whose votes were in the minority. Roberts's main argument concentrated on whether the decision about the legality of same-sex marriage "should rest with the people acting through their elected representatives" or with the Supreme Court justices.

He noted that marriage is not mentioned in the Constitution. For that reason, the decision of whether or not to permit same-sex marriages was up to states and state voters. States had already permitted or banned same-sex

Rainbow-colored lights bathed the White House after same-sex marriage was legalized.

A Voice of Dissent

John G. Roberts Jr. was born in Buffalo, New York, in 1955. After graduating from Harvard Law School, he served as a law clerk in the Court of Appeals for the Second Circuit and then in the US Supreme Court. After working with the US Department of Justice and the White House, Roberts was appointed to the United States Court of Appeals for the District of Columbia Circuit in 2003.

After being nominated by President George W. Bush, Roberts became chief justice for the US Supreme Court on September 29, 2005. A chief justice is the judge who manages the other eight justices in the Supreme Court. As chief justice, Roberts chooses who writes the majority opinion when he sides with the majority. He has written many important decisions himself.

Chief Justice Roberts wrote the dissenting opinion in *Obergefell*.

Roberts has recommended that the Supreme Court exercise restraint in its rulings. In other words, he has warned the court about overstepping. He believes the president and Congress should set the direction for change in the country. Roberts clearly expressed that belief in his dissenting opinion for *Obergefell v. Hodges*. He used strongly worded language to state that the Supreme Court should interpret rather than create laws.

marriage. He argued that "under the Constitution, judges have power to say what the law is, not what it should be." In other words, he felt as though it was not the Supreme Court's right to create laws. He thought this power only belonged to the states and state representatives in Congress.

Roberts believed that the five justices who voted in favor of same-sex marriage wanted to "remake society." He believed that they interpreted the Fourteenth Amendment too broadly. He thought that they took power out of the hands of voters in the states that did not want to legalize same-sex marriages. "The majority's decision is an act of will, not legal judgment," Roberts wrote. He criticized the majority for overstepping its bounds.

Justice Roberts also mentioned examples of marriage being defined as a union between a man and woman. He wrote that even the earlier case *Loving v. Virginia* did not change this "core meaning of marriage." Roberts also questioned "why the two-person element of the core definition of marriage may be preserved while the man-woman element may not." In other words, he wondered what would stop polygamy, or being married to more than one person at the same time, from being legalized now that same-sex marriage was legal.

Roberts concluded:

> If you are among the many Americans ... who favor expanding same-sex marriage, by all means celebrate today's decision. Celebrate the achievement of a desired goal. Celebrate the opportunity for a new expression of commitment to a partner. Celebrate the availability of new benefits. But do not celebrate the Constitution. It had nothing to do with it. I respectfully dissent.

In other words, he suggested that while supporters of same-sex marriage could celebrate their victory in court, there was no legal basis for it. He felt the court's decision was not in line with the Constitution.

Other Justices Dissent

The other three justices who did not support the court's decision supported Chief Justice Roberts's dissenting opinion. They all also wrote their own dissenting opinions. Each one explained why they did not vote in favor of the plaintiffs.

Justice Antonin Scalia stated in plain language that he thought the Supreme Court had gone too far in making its decision. Scalia wrote that it was "not of special importance … what the law says about marriage." In other words, he was not particularly concerned with what the Constitution said about marriage. Scalia was more concerned with how the decision had been made. He believed that the decision signaled to the public that the "majority of the nine lawyers on the Supreme Court" were in power. In Scalia's view, the decision "robs the People of … the freedom to govern themselves." Scalia believed this decision took the power away from the people.

Justice Samuel Alito agreed. He believed the justices had overstepped.

Justice Clarence Thomas took a slightly different approach in his opinion. He believed that same-sex marriage should not be compared to interracial marriage. "The suggestion …is both offensive and inaccurate," he wrote. He discussed how the laws against interracial marriage were rooted in slavery. He argued that "laws defining marriage as between one man and one woman do not share this sordid history." For that reason, he did not believe the comparison was fair. He also believed that "the traditional definition of marriage has prevailed in every society that has recognized marriage throughout history." In other words, he believed that people everywhere understood marriage to be between a man and a woman.

Aftermath

It had been a long, tough road toward recognition, but Jim Obergefell had finally won. After the verdict was announced, Obergefell said, "Today's ruling from the Supreme Court affirms what millions across the country already know to be true in our hearts: that our love is equal." In other words, he was hoping that the decision confirmed to all that everyone's love should be recognized equally. He also went on to say that he hoped "that the term gay marriage will soon be a thing of the past." He hoped "that from this day forward it will be, simply, marriage."

However, people's opinions across America were far from unanimous. While the plaintiffs may have won their case in *Obergefell v. Hodges*, the struggle for equality in the United States was far from over.

FIVE

A Continuing Mission

The Supreme Court's ruling in *Obergefell v. Hodges* received strong reactions from both sides. Supporters of same-sex marriage celebrated. Those who disagreed felt betrayed by the legal system. They vowed to continue opposing the ruling.

Celebration

For those in favor of same-sex marriage, the verdict represented a victory after years of protest and struggle. Parades and celebrations popped up in cities across the nation. The United States joined twenty other countries that allowed same-sex marriages. The decision also led to a sudden increase in US same-sex marriages. More than one hundred thousand same-sex couples got married in the first year after *Obergefell*.

President Barack Obama said, "This ruling is a victory for America." He thought it was a win for the entire country because "when all Americans are truly treated as equal, we are more free." In other words, he believed Americans enjoyed more freedom when all Americans were treated equally.

Several months later, in spring 2016, President Obama gave a speech in which he said he was struck by the "rapidity

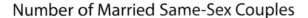

Number of Married Same-Sex Couples

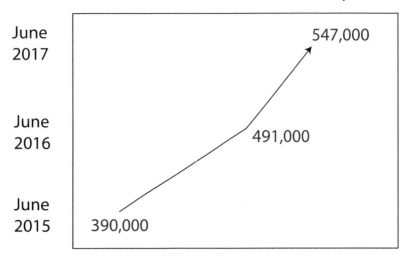

June 2017 — 547,000

June 2016 — 491,000

June 2015 — 390,000

The number of married same-sex couples increased rapidly after *Obergefell v. Hodges.*

with which the marriage equality movement changed the political landscape and hearts and minds." In other words, he was surprised by how quickly advocates for same-sex marriage had brought about real legal and social changes. He said that it was "probably … the fastest set of changes in terms of a social movement" that he had ever seen.

Shifts in Attitudes

It was certainly true that the situation had dramatically changed over a fairly short period of time.

Before 2004, no state allowed a marriage between two people of the same sex. By 2012, nine states as well as the District of Columbia had legalized same-sex marriage. After the *Windsor* ruling in 2013, many judges around the country began using that case as a precedent to rule in favor of same-sex marriages. By the time *Obergefell v. Hodges* was heard in the US Supreme Court, thirty-six states permitted same-sex marriages.

Public opinion had also moved from opposition to support. In 2001, only 35 percent of Americans approved of same-sex marriage, while 57 percent opposed. The remaining 8 percent of Americans were undecided. By 2014, the situation had reversed. Fifty-two percent of Americans were in favor of same-sex marriage, and 39 percent were against it. A 2017 poll showed even more people favored same-sex marriage. Sixty-two percent were in favor of it, while 32 percent remained opposed.

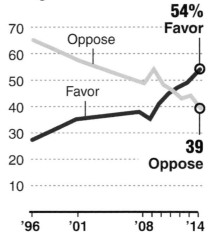

Views on gay marriage shift

How attitudes toward allowing gays and lesbians to marry legally have changed since 1996:

Polls show that the acceptance of same-sex marriage in the United States has grown over the years.

Religious Objections

While polls show that a majority of Americans now support same-sex marriage, nearly one-third of the nation's citizens still strongly opposed it as of 2017. Back in 1980, Reverend Jerry Falwell, the founder of a group called Moral Majority, said that "we would not be having the present moral crisis … if men and women accepted their proper roles as designated by God." In other words, Falwell believed that if men and women understood their traditional gender roles, then there would not be questions about who could marry whom.

Many religious leaders felt, and feel, the same way. Tony Perkins, president of the Family Research Council, has said that "no court can overturn nature's law." Perkins believes that it is against nature for people of the same sex to get married. Catholic Bishop Richard Malone stated that the idea of marriage being between one man and one woman "is rooted in creation." In other words, marriage between a man and a woman goes back to God creating Adam and Eve. Bishop Thomas Tobin called the *Obergefell* decision "an attempt to destroy God's plan." All of these religious leaders see the Supreme Court's ruling on same-sex marriage as a bad thing.

Despite the Supreme Court's ruling, many people continue to oppose same-sex marriage.

Split Along Party Lines

The timing of *Obergefell* made it a topic of discussion during the 2016 presidential election campaign. Many Republican candidates criticized the decision. Senator Marco Rubio of Florida said that he believed "marriage is between one man and one woman [and] if you disagree you should have the law changed by a legislature." Rubio supported a state's right to decide. Senator Ted Cruz of Texas called *Obergefell* one of "the darkest hours in our nation's history."

Same-sex marriage remained an issue in the 2016 presidential election, with most Republican candidates saying they were against it.

On the other hand, Democratic candidate Hillary Clinton criticized her Republican opponents. She thought that they should be celebrating the end of this "discrimination once and for all."

Senator Bernie Sanders of Vermont felt similarly. He stated that "this decision is a victory for same-sex couples across our country as well as all those seeking to live in a nation where every citizen is afforded equal rights."

Politicians and State Officials Weigh In

Politicians have also made their views known. In Congress, most Democrats considered *Obergefell v. Hodges* to be a victory for civil rights. On the other hand, many Republicans criticized the Supreme Court for ruling against local laws and voters in their states.

After the Supreme Court legalized same-sex marriage, most states announced that they intended to follow the law. Attorney General Jim Hood of Mississippi ordered county clerks to approve same-sex marriages. He said that it was now "the law of the land."

However, some local government officials in several states refused to obey. In the months following the ruling, several counties in Alabama, Kentucky, and Texas refused to issue marriage licenses to same-sex couples. One clerk quit rather than issue a license. Another clerk went to jail for disobeying the new law. In Alabama, since early 2015, eight counties tried to avoid recognizing same-sex marriages by refusing to grant marriage licenses to any couple.

Proposed Alternatives

Some people are attempting to bridge the gap between supporters and opponents to same-sex marriage. These people have proposed that there could be other forms of legal arrangements for same-sex couples. They suggest civil unions or domestic partnerships that could grant same-sex couples similar, if not identical, rights. These alternatives existed before the legalization of same-sex marriages.

However, the rules that define these arrangements can vary from one state to the next. They also fail to provide the same federal benefits as legal marriages. Additionally, the federal government does not recognize them.

Most important, many same-sex couples object to these kinds of proposals. They are not looking for an arrangement that is "close" or "similar" to marriage. They want full acceptance and recognition of their relationships just like opposite-sex couples.

Future Threats

While the Supreme Court did legalize same-sex marriage in *Obergefell v. Hodges*, the vote was close (5–4). The four dissenting justices harshly criticized the decision. As long as the five justices that voted for the plaintiffs remain on the court, their decision is likely to stand. However, the make-up of the court will eventually change.

Supreme Court justices can serve for life. When a Supreme Court justice dies or retires, the president of the United States nominates a replacement. The replacement must then be confirmed by the US Senate. For example, Justice Neil Gorsuch joined the Supreme Court in April 2017. He was nominated and confirmed after Justice Antonin Scalia passed away in February 2016. Gorsuch's views appear to be similar to Scalia's. However, another change in the court could lead to a shift in opinions about same-sex marriage. Another case could arise with new justices that could lead to a different understanding of marriage rights and equality in the United States.

Other Ways to Discriminate

Even if *Obergefell* remains in place, that case only dealt with the issue of same-sex marriage. After the Supreme Court's decision, some states passed laws that discriminated against the LGBTQ community in other ways. For instance,

Alabama created laws that allow adoption agencies to discriminate against same-sex couples. Similar laws have been created in South Dakota, North Dakota, Michigan, Texas, and Virginia. Even though same sex-marriage has been legalized, people still stand in the way of same-sex couples being treated equally.

Obergefell Continues the Fight

Jim Obergefell's pursuit of equal treatment for all people continues. He travels around the country speaking about civil rights. He recently coauthored a book, *Love Wins: The Lovers and Lawyers Who Fought the Landmark Case for Marriage Equality*. The book tells his and John Arthur's story.

Jim Obergefell and others continue to fight for equal rights.

In the years since his Supreme Court case, Obergefell has won many awards from organizations such as Equality Florida and the Ohio Democratic Party. In June 2017, Obergefell received another honor. The city of Cincinnati renamed a city street "John Arthur and Jim Obergefell Way" in honor of Obergefell and his late husband.

The *Washington Post* once called Obergefell "the face of the Supreme Court gay marriage case." National Public Radio (NPR) referred to him as "the name that will go down in history." For Jim Obergefell, however, it was really just about gaining equal acceptance and recognition of his love for John Arthur.

Who has the right to marry? How do we define "family"? *Obergefell v. Hodges* helped to answer some of those fundamental questions. Along with his legal team and his many supporters, Jim Obergefell helped to change the laws and the opinions of a nation. His work and the work of the LGBTQ community continues.

Chronology

1868 The Fourteenth Amendment to the US Constitution provides equal protection to all US citizens.

1967 The US Supreme Court rules that Virginia's law against interracial marriage is unconstitutional (*Loving v. Virginia*).

1972 The US Supreme Court declines to consider a case concerning two men who are refused a marriage license in Minnesota (*Baker v. Nelson*).

1973 Maryland is the first state to ban same-sex marriage.

1996 Congress passes the Defense of Marriage Act (DOMA), which prevents the US government from recognizing same-sex marriages performed in any state or country.

2004 Based on a 2003 court ruling (*Goodridge v. Department of Public Health*), Massachusetts becomes the first state to legalize same-sex marriage.

2013 The Supreme Court strikes down part of DOMA (*United States v. Windsor*) and overturns California's Proposition 8, which banned same-sex marriage (*Hollingsworth v. Perry*). Maryland legalizes same-sex marriage.

Same-Sex Marriage:
Obergefell v. Hodges

2014 The Court of Appeals for the Sixth Circuit overturns district court decisions in *Obergefell v. Hodges*, *Bourke v. Beshear*, *Tanco v. Haslam*, and *DeBeor v. Snyder*. Lawyers for Obergefell file a petition with the US Supreme Court.

2015 The Supreme Court legalizes same-sex marriage in the United States (*Obergefell v. Hodges*).

2017 The US Supreme Court reverses an Arkansas Supreme Court decision that prevented same-sex married couples from having both spouses' names listed on their children's birth certificates (*Pavan v. Smith*).

Glossary

amended Made changes in a legal document to add or revise information.

appeal To ask a higher court to change the ruling of a lower court.

cited Mentioned something (a document or quote) as proof or evidence to support an argument.

civil rights The rights that people have in a society.

defendants People being sued or accused of a crime in a court of law.

discrimination Unfair treatment of people based on a part of their identity, such as age, race, or gender.

dissenting opinion A written explanation by a judge who disagrees with the majority decision in a case.

federal government The central US government.

gay A term used to refer to homosexuals (usually men).

GLBTQ (or LGBTQ) An acronym that stands for gay, lesbian, bisexual, transgender, and queer.

heterosexuals People who are attracted to those of the opposite sex.

homosexuals People who are attracted to those of the same sex.

majority opinion The written explanation for a decision that is agreed to by more than half of the judges of a court.

petitioners People who make a formal request to a court.

plaintiffs People who bring a case against other people (defendants) in a court of law.

precedent A decision in an earlier legal case that is used as an example or guide to make a decision in a similar case at a later time.

stays Short delays ordered by judges in court cases to give the defendant time before obeying the court's decision.

swing vote The vote that decides a close case that could "swing" one way or the other.

unconstitutional A law or action that does not follow the rules of the US Constitution.

uphold When judges say that an earlier decision was correct.

Further Information

Books

Andryszewski, Tricia. *Same-Sex Marriage: Granting Equal Rights or Damaging the Status of Marriage?* Minneapolis: Twenty-First Century Books, 2012.

Newton, David E. *Same-Sex Marriage: A Reference Handbook.* Contemporary World Issues. Santa Barbara, CA: ABC-CLIO, 2010.

Porterfield, Jason. *Marriage Equality: Obergefell v. Hodges.* US Supreme Court Landmark Cases. New York: Enslow Publishing, 2017.

Stone, Geoffrey. R. *Sex and the Constitution: Sex, Religion, and Law from America's Origins to the Twenty-First Century.* New York: Liveright Publishing Corporation, 2017.

Websites

Keppler Speakers: Jim Obergefell
https://www.kepplerspeakers.com/speakers/jim-obergefell/videos

This website includes several short video interviews in which Obergefell talks about the Supreme Court case and how important it is to keep working to protect people's equal rights.

Pew Research Center

http://www.pewresearch.org

The Pew Research Center provides information about important issues, attitudes, and trends that affect the world while avoiding taking sides on any topic.

Supreme Court of the United States

https://www.supremecourt.gov

The government website for the US Supreme Court includes everything you might want to know about the court, its justices, its opinions, and its schedule.

Videos

"Lawyer Mary Bonauto Remarks on the Supreme Court Ruling on Same-Sex Marriage"

https://www.c-span.org/video/?c4542179/lawyer-mary-bonauto-remarks-supreme-court-ruling-marriage

This is a video of Mary Bonauto's comments after the Supreme Court's ruling.

"Supreme Court: Marriage Is a Fundamental Right for Gay Couples"

https://www.cbsnews.com/news/supreme-court-marriage-is-a-fundamental-right-for-gay-couples

This video gives a brief recap of the *Obergefell v. Hodges* decision and the initial public reactions.

"Video Clip: Obergefell v Hodges."

https://www.c-span.org/classroom/document/?6298

This is a video of Jim Obergefell discussing the Supreme Court decision.

Selected Bibliography

Barbash, Fred, Mark Berman, and Sandhya Somashekhar. "Supreme Court Hears Same-Sex Marriage Case: Who Said What (with Audio)." *Washington Post*, April 28, 2015. https://www.washingtonpost.com/news/post-nation/wp/2015/04/28/supreme-court-hears-arguments-in-same-sex-marriage-case-obergefell-v-hodges-today/?utm_term=.6fbcedced47b.

"Changing Attitudes on Gay Marriage." Pew Research Center, June 26, 2017. http://www.pewforum.org/fact-sheet/changing-attitudes-on-gay-marriage.

de Vogue, Ariane. "Meet the Lawyers Who Will Argue the Gay Marriage Case." CNN, April 27, 2015. http://www.cnn.com/2015/04/24/politics/supreme-court-gay-marriage-lawyers/index.html.

Gabel-Brett, Leslie J., and Kevin M. Cathcart. "Introduction: Love Unites Us." In *Love Unites Us: Winning The Freedom To Marry in America,* edited by Kevin M. Cathcart and Leslie J. Gabel-Brett, 1–18. New York: The New Press, 2016.

Gates, Gary J., and Taylor N. T. Brown. "Marriage and Same-Sex Couples After *Obergefell*." The Williams Institute, November 2015. https://williamsinstitute.law.ucla.edu/

wp-content/uploads/Marriage-and-Same-sex-Couples-after-Obergefell-November-2015.pdf.

"John G. Roberts, Jr." Oyez. Accessed December 27, 2017. https://www.oyez.org/justices/john_g_roberts_jr.

Liptak, Adam. "Supreme Court Ruling Makes Same-Sex Marriage a Right Nationwide." *New York Times*, June 26, 2015. https://www.nytimes.com/2015/06/27/us/supreme-court-same-sex-marriage.html.

"Local Government Responses to *Obergefell v. Hodges*." Ballotpedia, June 26, 2017. https://ballotpedia.org/Local_government_responses_to_Obergefell_v._Hodges.

"Loving v. Virginia." Oyez. Accessed December 9, 2017. https://www.oyez.org/cases/1966/395.

"Obergefell v. Hodges." ACLU Ohio. Accessed December 15, 2017. http://www.acluohio.org/archives/cases/obergefell-v-hodges.

"Obergefell v. Hodges." Ballotpedia. Accessed December 10, 2017. https://ballotpedia.org/Obergefell_v._Hodges#Case_background.

"Obergefell v. Hodges, et al. (U.S. Sup. Ct.)." Constitutional Accountability Center. Accessed December 10, 2017. https://www.theusconstitution.org/cases/obergefell-v-hodges-et-al-us-sup-ct.

"Obergefell v. Hodges, 576 U.S. (2015)." Justia. Accessed December 4, 2017. https://supreme.justia.com/cases/federal/us/576/14-556.

"Sanders Statement on Supreme Court Decision on Same-Sex Marriage." Bernie Sanders: U.S. Senator for Vermont, June 26, 2015. https://www.sanders.senate.gov/newsroom/press-releases/sanders-statement-on-supreme-court-decision-on-same-sex-marriage.

Schwartz, John. "Obergefell v. Hodges: Highlights from the Supreme Court Decision on Same-Sex Marriage." *New York Times*, June 8, 2015. https://www.nytimes.com/interactive/2015/us/2014-term-supreme-court-decision-same-sex-marriage.html?_r=1.

Valencia, Milton. J. "Mary Bonauto Reflects on the Year Since Supreme Court's Gay-Marriage Ruling." *Boston Globe*, June 27, 2016. https://www.bostonglobe.com/metro/2016/06/27/mary-bonauto-reflects-anniversary-gay-marriage-ruling/z7zedQjR8aqP8Ny0dLPcLM/story.html.

"Visitors Guide to Oral Argument." Supreme Court. Accessed December 11, 2017. https://www.supremecourt.gov/visiting/visitorsguidetooralargument.aspx.

"Watch Unreleased Footage of Obama's Phone Call to James Obergefell on the Night of the Supreme Court's Same-Sex Marriage Decision." *Washington Post*, August 16, 2016. https://www.washingtonpost.com/graphics/national/obama-legacy/gay-marriage-stance.html.

Index

About the Author

Gerry Boehme is an author, editor, and speaker who lives in New York. He loves to travel and to learn about new things. He especially enjoys talking with people who have different backgrounds and opinions. Gerry has written books for students dealing with many subjects, including *Edward Snowden: Heroic Whistleblower or Traitorous Spy?*, *John Lewis and Desegregation*, *Heresy: The Spanish Inquisition*, and *Roberto Clemente: The Pride of Puerto Rico*.